A short story about Autism
Pedro's Visit to the Aquarium

Written by: Rasheedah Saleem-Muhammad

Illustrated by: Crystal Harris

First published by Dog Ear Publishing
4010 W. 86th Street, Ste H
Indianapolis, IN 46268
www.dogearpublishing.net

dog ear PUBLISHING

ISBN: 978-160844-426-7

This book is printed on acid-free paper.

Printed in the United States of America

Pedro is an seven year old little boy who has been diagnosed with autism (a developmental disorder that makes it hard for him to communicate with others). He attends a large school in the state of New Jersey. This big school has students who are in special classes like Pedro and some students who are not in special classes. There are six students in his classroom.

Aa Bb Cc Dd Ee
1 2 3 4 5 6 7 8 9 10 11 12 13 14 15

Pedro can learn like other children his age. But, at times he needs additional help. He has a helper to make sure he understands what the teacher is saying. Pedro is friendly, loves to write, play and sing. Pedro loves to sing rhythm and blues (R&B) music. His favorite artists are Michael Jackson, Beyonce, Alicia Keys, Taylor Swift, Shakira and Mary J. Blige. Pedro also likes to sing the theme music from the Steve Harvey morning show and Old MacDonald.

Alicia

Sometimes, Pedro's disorder makes him become silly and emotional. He will cry at the drop of a dime; especially when he thinks of his favorite underwater, yellow cartoon character. If Pedro sees anything that resembles characters from this popular television show he yells, screams or kicks with excitement, which sometimes turns into frustration for the adults around Pedro. At times, it is extremely difficult for adults to help Pedro become calm.

Because Pedro is so emotional and sometimes gets excited, his parents are afraid to take him to certain places like the supermarket or the shopping mall. They are afraid the crowds will excite him. Sometimes Pedro's parents are embarrassed by his behavior. "I feel like everyone is looking at us and they do not know what I am going through or how I feel," his mom would state. She often stated that she wanted to tell the crowd of witnesses that Pedro is autistic! Mom also notices that Pedro's behavior is much different at school than at home, Pedro was much more excited at home. His parents did not know if they should give into his behavior or just be firm.

TO THE MALL

His parents also know that they could not go into the stores and remove all of the yellow cartoon character items off the shelves or take every backpack or tee-shirts off children as they walked through the stores. His mother spoke to his teacher and they immediately began to work on correcting Pedro's not so good behavior. A good manners plan and a reward token system were included into his daily schedule.

With the support of his family, classroom teachers and weeks of hard work Pedro was ready to test his new skills. He was shown pictures of crowded, busy places such as, the carnival and the movie theater.

Pedro's teacher informed the class that they were going on a field trip to the Rainbow Water Aquarium. Pedro looked forward to the class trip. He knows his favorite cartoon character lives in the water. Before visiting the aquarium Pedro and the class were introduced to the various animals they would see while visiting the aquarium. The class also got the opportunity to watch the movie "Finding Nemo", which was an all time class favorite.

Science

On the day of the trip, the teacher and Pedro's parents explained to him that he would visit the water mammals that he had been learning about in class. Pedro was shown pictures on the exact aquarium so that it was not a shock to him. At times, Pedro doesn't know how to handle change. The day of the trip he was shown a variety of pictures so there would be as few outbursts as possible.

Pedro
Rainbow Aquarium

The bus ride to the aquarium was less than one hour which was great. He did not become restless. Pedro asked questions about the aquarium prior to the class arrival. Once the class arrived Pedro was on his best behavior.

He had some of his favorite activities and toys with him to keep him busy. He sat appropriately while the aquarium staff asked questions and explained the sea creatures. He was quiet and kept his hands to himself. Pedro was completely amazed by all the different animals he saw.

GUIDE

When Pedro saw a horseshoe crab, he immediately thought about his favorite television character and started to cry. He was screaming and drew attention to himself. His teacher and a classroom helper came to his rescue. They began to sing his favorite song, "Old Mac Donald" and lightly stroked his back to calm him. Pedro had one outburst during the entire trip.

Upon returning back to the school, Pedro asked his teacher many questions about the aquarium. He stated "I am going to tell mommy and daddy about the trip"! When the bus arrived back to the school Pedro's parents were anxiously waiting. They had puzzled looks on their faces. They were nervous about his behavior and thought maybe visiting the aquarium was not a good idea, because of Pedro's strong obsession with the cartoon character and the water. After hearing about Pedro's day his parents were filled with joy. They were happy; they faced their fears by deciding to let him go on the class trip to the aquarium.

Care Cruiser

Mommy immediately thought with the proper training and dedication they could begin taking Pedro on more family outings. They know they would have to start taking small steps, and gradually increase the time.

Pedro's parents were happy with the progress he made and from that day forward, they knew Pedro could do things that other children his age were doing. Later that year, Pedro went to summer camp and took a family vacation with his parents.

LaVergne, TN USA
08 June 2010
185369LV00002B

* 9 7 8 1 6 0 8 4 4 4 2 6 7 *